ALICIA CHMIELEWSKI

Pause and Smile

A Little Guide to Finding Happiness Even in Tough Times

First edition

This book was professionally typeset on Reedsy.
Find out more at reedsy.com

This book is dedicated to my friends, family, acquaintances and strangers.
Regardless of what challenges you face,
may you always find an abundance of reasons to smile.

Contents

Introduction

As I sit here writing, I look to my left and see movement under a red and white plaid blanket thrown about over the ottoman in my living room. My heart is filled with joy as I know that something so sweet and gentle is making herself warm and cozy. My little Mili. The younger of my two fur babies. Yes they drive me crazy from time-to-time, especially when walking in front of my computer when I'm trying to work, yet I can't imagine loving any little balls of fluff more.

Isn't it funny how happiness and smiles can be found in such simple ways? As humans, we tend to place such an emphasis on the negative in our lives that we forget what's really important, and how simple it really is to be happy, and to share our happiness with others.

I'm no doctor, scientist, or guru but one thing's for sure, I am overall a generally happy person. Optimistic, yet realistic. While I have my moments, my glass is usually "half full." I've definitely had my share of heartbreaks, setbacks, failures, and disappointments; yet, overcoming and moving on is paramount, as those negative feelings can really be a drag literally preventing one from accomplishing and enjoying so, very much in life.

Everyone experiences sadness and its sometimes quite hard to recover. It is my mission to not only share my journey, but inspire others to find their happy, their smile, once again.

Heartbreak to Restored Faith

t what moment did I know things were going to be okay in my life you may wonder? Sit back, relax and let me take you on a journey. The journey that gave me the message that I'd be alright and that I should and could have faith and trust.

It was a horrible time. I had made the hardest decision to that point in my life, and that decision was to walk away from my marriage and leave everything so that I could start anew.

I didn't "have-it-all," but we had just recently remodeled our house exactly the way I'd wanted. I'd refurnished our home with beautiful traditionally inspired pieces. I personally designed and built my own mini "Garden of Eden," in my backyard. Seriously, it was gorgeous! Everyone loved to come and sit amid the flowering plants, while the little tortoises that enjoyed my beautiful masterpiece of a garden for years walked up to greet them. The properties that we'd acquired. Remodeled. Demoed. Yada yada yada. Stuff. The robot vacuum, the cool new dryer, the kitchen knickknacks that are so useful those few times you ever actually need to use them. I left it all, my pets, everything. I said goodbye to the softest linens that I so loved, the comforts of home and my stuff. Literally, I took one paycheck, rented an apartment and filed for divorce. More than stuff, I wanted to find myself and my joy that had somehow slipped away off into the abyss. I wanted to start over. I needed to be free. I took my clothes, 4 serving sets, the bedroom set I had since I lived at home with my parents and left for good.

Let's make one thing clear, this was not a happy-go-lucky time of my life. Each day was filled with worry, doubt, uncertainty, and usually some tears too.

I knew deep down that I'd made the hardest, yet best decision for me to that point in my life. I was filled with fear. I never *had* to provide for myself, heck, I didn't even know if I could. My business was okay, not incredible, by not bad either. My big worry was, "Could I do it on my own?" One thing was for sure, the fear was real! The what-if's plagued my mind but I knew deep down that I was going to have to face my fears if I were to find joy in my life again. The smiles everyone saw on my face were fake. So very fake.

I'll never forget the day I cried myself home, not knowing if I'd be able to make my car payment, rent, or pretty much pay anything. I had a lot of business in the works but while being 100% commission there's nothing steady or predictable financially about that. I worked my open house, showed homes to clients, and drove home. With tears filling my eyes, I prayed to God, and prayed and prayed. "Why doesn't God speak to me like other people?" I wondered. I'm a Christian but let's face it, I've never heard a booming voice or any voice for that matter reply to me when in prayer. "Why does God talk to everyone else but me?," I remembered thinking. "Maybe He doesn't speak and so many of these Christian believers are liars." How would I make it through this time of fear by myself?

Financially I didn't have anyone to lean on or help if I needed it. I was convinced that I had no friends that really cared. I was entirely and utterly alone. Would I even make it before becoming homeless? Who could I talk to? I know deep down that God is, was and always will be there but he never chatted back when I talked to Him. I was at an utter loss. Bawling my eyes out, I prayed. "God, if you're there listening, give me a sign. Speak to me Lord. Let me know what I need to do. Let me know that I'll somehow make it. Not only do I need money, I need to know that I can take care of myself and survive!"

It was a cloudy day with a very ominous looking sky. It wasn't raining, but it looked like it could at any moment. The clouds parted just enough to create what looked like a spotlight over where my little apartment and neighborhood now was. I was still a few miles from home but the sky had me a bit distracted. It seemed funny how that "spotlight" appeared to be directly over my neighborhood. Mesmerized may have been a more apropos word.

As I prayed, I listened to the classical crossover piano music playing on repeat as I drove. The fact that the music didn't have vocals, made it easier for me to focus but that sky was more captivating than the road. Looking back, if I were a police officer I would have pulled myself over thinking I was a danger to myself and anyone else on the road considering I bumped into the curb. But come on, with all the tears in my eyes it was hard to see, and that sky! I kept praying "Lord please let me know I'm going to be okay!"

Funny enough, a thought popped into my head. I thought of the message in the Bible where Jesus speaks to his disciples and says that the blackbirds don't worry about where their next meal comes from yet they still eat and that God loves us so much more than the birds. Yes, I thought. I vaguely remember that message from Sunday School when

I was a little girl. While it was cute I thought of that out of the blue, I needed to focus on my talk with God who was obviously not "speaking". So, I continued driving and crying.

As I got closer to home I saw more and more "spotlights" appearing in the sky. So many that It was absolutely mesmerizing. It was as though as far as I could see was a stage. Think of the coolest show or concert you've ever been to with great light effects and tons of spotlights - now multiply that by one hundred. I wanted to pull off the road somewhere that I'd be able to see them all. My view was a bit obstructed with the tons of roof tops in my way blocking the sky yet, I remembered a pond in the back of my neighborhood that I adored walking to and watching the sunset over. I loved this area because there wasn't any rooftops or buildings that would impede my view. I drove there. I parked my car and kept praying, crying and listening to my music.

"God, I'm not kidding, I need a sign that I'm going to be okay!" I prayed. Where was the big booming voice? Nowhere. A little tiny voice? Nope, I didn't hear that either. I did; however, notice the big black and yellow arrow sign in front of my car before the pond. You know the one that signals to drivers that if you don't turn left as the road bends you'll wind up in the water. I chuckled as I thought yeah right. "I pulled up to this sign, God. You didn't put it here knowing I was on the way. It's been here as long as I was aware of this spot."

By this point I have few tears left to cry so I'm just sitting there staring at the rays of sunlight that are piercing the clouds in such great abundance. Words truly can't describe the majesty of the sky that day. It was incredible, awe inspiring, absolutely wondrous!

The bird story from Sunday School years ago returned to my mind. I may have even rolled my eyes thinking how I didn't feel as special or as loved as a bird at that point. Then something profound happened. A bird landed on the tree branch right in front of me. I know what you're probably thinking: Birds land in trees all day long. In most cases, I would have thought the same; yet, I didn't this time. Why? Because I'd never seen a bird like this. Even to this day, I'd never seen one with these colors, and haven't since.

This bird was a black bird with a brilliant yellow head and chest. This bird landed on the tree that the arrow sign was pointing directly toward and with the exact colors of that sign. I couldn't believe it. It was gorgeous and everything was so perfectly matching between that sign and the bird's colors!

It was almost as though God was saying, "How much more obvious do you want these signs?! I've made it abundantly clear but here's one more *sign* for you since you missed all the others."

It was at that moment that I knew, beyond a shadow of a doubt, that my prayers were heard and everything that had occurred since I began praying was all a sign. God wasn't speaking in an audible voice. I asked for signs and that's what I received.

- Light in the darkness.
- The black birds never need to worry about their next meal yet they always have food. God provides and He loves his children so much more than the birds.
- If the actual yellow and black arrow sign wasn't enough, the fact that the bird that landed on the branch the arrow pointing too was matching in color.

* * *

Luke 12:22-31 NIV

Then Jesus said to his disciples: "Therefore I tell you, do not worry about your life, what you will eat; or about your body, what you will wear. For life is more than food, and the body more than clothes. Consider the ravens: They do not sow or reap, they have no storeroom or barn; yet God feeds them. And how much more valuable you are than birds! Who of you by worrying can add a single hour to your life? Since you cannot do this very little thing, why do you worry about the rest?

Consider how the wild flowers grow. They do not labor or spin. Yet I tell you, not even Solomon in all his splendor was dressed like one of these. If that is how God clothes the grass of the field, which is here today, and tomorrow is thrown into the fire, how much more will he clothe you—you of little faith! And do not set your heart on what you will eat or drink; do not worry about it. For the pagan world runs after all such things, and your Father knows that you need them. But seek his kingdom, and these things will be given to you as well."

* * *

It was then that everything came together in my mind and I knew, even though I didn't know how, I knew I was going to be okay. It wasn't just a little feeling; it was an absolute, undeniable, unwavering, kind of confidence that swept over me. My faith had been restored! God really does love His children after all. Even me! Even when I felt so heartbroken, alone and unloved.

It was that moment that my confidence was made new and I was 100%

sure that I was going to make it. I was going to be okay.

The weight I felt on my shoulders began lessening. Troubles began lifting. What once felt like roadblocks and challenges slowly became smoother. Was it God working? Was it just me pushing forward and not giving up? Was it my newfound confidence manifesting outcomes? I believe the answer is an absolute yes to all the above.

I still get chills to this day recollecting this moment. It was one of those few life changing experiences that can completely alter the course of your mind, spirit, self-peace and nearly every aspect of life. My new chapter was beginning and although I didn't know who, what, when, where, why or how, I knew I was heading in the right direction.

Life Now

Has life been perfect since? No. The message I received that day was the trigger that made me start focusing and practicing finding the good in my daily life. I gave myself little assignments which really helped turn things around and train my mind in positive thinking. Having the confidence and faith that everything would be okay was the baseline for sure.

Finding your smile in situations and in daily life can be a challenge for all of us, but when you start practicing and focusing on them it seams like you have more and more. Let me rephrase that, it doesn't just *seem like,* you WILL experience more and more happiness.

"What you focus on expands." is not a joke. Whoever the wise person was that came up with this saying, came up with a law for life. This truth has been proven time and time again by people all around the world. If you focus on negative people or situations you'll have more of them in your life. If you focus on the positive, you'll have more happiness as you experience life. Who wouldn't want to be happier?

Not every day will be perfect. Not every moment will be joyous, yet some will be. The more you focus on the happy, the more self-peace you'll have and happier you'll become.

It is my sincere hope and wish that by sharing my story, you are encouraged and realize what I did; God is watching out for all his creation, even you and me. He always has, and always will be there, even when we feel like we're standing alone. Trust Him!

Whatever you've been through or are going through, know that light will shine through the darkness and better, happier moments are ahead for you. Discovering them and being open to receiving them is what we're going to work on next.

Consider Your Environment

I t's amazing how much of ourselves is influenced by our surroundings. Have you been to a nice place and just breathed in the beauty of your environment? Maybe it's a garden that's blossoming with the sweetest smelling flowers. How heavenly! How do you feel in a place like this?

Now envision the opposite. A negative place that you may be fearful or turned off by. If this place was filled with condescending people, danger, discomfort would you find yourself smiling like you may in the beautiful garden?

Laying in bed wallowing in one's thoughts isn't going to change any mindsets or make any moods better. You absolutely must change your environment to inspire change in your spirit. It doesn't have to be permanent but just remember that everything, everyone, and every thought, every piece of music you let in your space effects you. For this reason, distance yourself from environments, people and situations that weigh on your spirit.

Where is your happy place? How often do you visit? Is it time to spend some time there now?

Have you noticed that your taste in music changes depending upon your mood? Many people do. If your spirit is peaceful you might listen to more melodic music. Alternatively, when you're angry you might prefer to listen to harsher sounds.

What would happen if we change something as subtle as what we listen to in the car while driving from point A to point B? Would that influence our mood? You bet!

This Guide

Take a deep breath, relax and focus on your whole self. Slow the racing thoughts in your mind and ground yourself into the present. Everything can wait. This is your time.

As you begin, you'll notice that each self-reminder exercise is on it's own page. This was intentional. Focus on that page and only that page and the moment that comes to mind. Some will use this as a meditation per day. This is an excellent practice and you'll be pleased to know that there's thirty-one so each day of the month has it's own self-reminder.

This is not the time to speed read your way through, but rather to fully focus on and embrace the emotions and memories of the moments that come to mind. This is the time to recollect, smile, remember and perhaps even reach out to the person or people that come to mind to share that you were thinking of them if someone was, involved in the memory.

Bask in the senses that you recall and fully embrace the memory until that moment passes. How does this memory make you feel? For a moment envision all the senses that were felt. Was it a warm sunny day? Maybe your skin felt warm. Flowers blooming nearby? Perhaps you recall their sweet scent that filled the air. Did you embrace someone? If so, envision the bond you shared, a tender touch and the entire moment that transpired. Were you eating something? Was it delicious? Can you remember the taste and your initial response the moment you took your first bite? What did you see? Was it a pleasant sight? Silly? Surprising? Did you hear anything? Perhaps you were in a park and heard children playing or birds singing. Take it all in. Was there a lesson to be learned? Maybe simply nothing at all. Embrace it and all the emotions that come with that memory.

If you journal, or are even considering starting, you'll find each the perfect guide to base your writing on. If writing isn't your thing, that's okay too. Meditate or simply focus on the thought at hand.

It's okay to laugh, it's okay to cry, it's okay to smile just simply be in the moment for a while. Do you miss this moment? That's okay too. The point to this exercise or meditation is to simply remind ourselves how much we have to be thankful for.

Each moment happened once. There will never be an exact duplicate so don't get hung up on wishing for a repeat. Embrace it for the singular moment it was. If you're a believer, thank God for the moment and the positive impact that it had on your life. Have gratitude and feel the thankfulness for that memory in your heart.

Then know, although you'll never have this same moment again, you will have new moments that are also memorable, maybe even more-so. Your response to these questions may change tomorrow, next week, next month or next year. That's okay. In fact, that's excellent! That means that you're living an abundant life and treasuring so many experiences. This guide wasn't designed to be a race to the end, only to be placed on a shelf to collect dust. This is a living guide where your answer will likely change. When you make it through each exercise, go back and begin again, perhaps prefacing the self-reminder to a memory that occurred in the last day, week, month, etc.

What's fun is to go back and review your journal entry for each memory in the future. For that it's recommended that you actually keep a written journal. In a few years, read your answers and see just how far you and your happy life experiences has changed and evolved.

Without distractions, with a quiet mind, and a heart of gratitude, you're ready to begin.

Self-Reminders to Ponder

L et's begin with an example:

Imagine a piece of music that brings immense joy to your heart. What is it? Where does the memory take you?

The piece of music that I think of is Pachelbel's Cannon. My mother would practice piano after I was put to bed as a little girl. I just loved hearing her play that piece. It was like every inch of my being was taken by the music's beauty and I simply wanted to float in joy.

I giggle reminiscing about these moments. Every time she'd play it I would get out of bed and dance around my bedroom. If I was lucky I wouldn't get caught by Dad who would tell me it's past my bedtime and that I needed to go back to bed. I smile now because I know there wasn't one time Mom played that piece, when I was not yet asleep, that I didn't get up and dance. (That's right Dad, even when you thought I was sleeping I was dancing!) To this day, as a full grown adult, even if I don't physically get up to dance my heart still does, and you'll often find me smiling when I hear this piece.

Now it's your turn.

Day 1

Imagine a piece of music that brings immense joy to your heart.

What is it?

Where does the memory take you?

Day 2

Think about a moment this week that someone said something you weren't expecting that made you smile.

What was it?

Who said it?

Where were you?

Recreate it in your mind.

Are you smiling?

Day 3

Think about something you did this week that made someone else smile.

What where the circumstances?

Who's life did you positively impact with a smile as a result of what you said or did?

Day 4

I magine that you're visiting the most beautiful place you've ever been.

Where are you?

What does it feel like to be in this place?

Are you warm or cool?

How do you feel?

Day 5

Remember a time that you thought about giving up but then pressed onward.

You weren't comfortable, maybe frightened, maybe even terrified, but you pushed on and achieved what you nearly gave up on.

What was it?

You are so brave for pushing past the uncomfortable!

Day 6

Isn't seeing a rainbow glorious?!

Without rain, rainbows wouldn't exist; much like how without darkness, there would be no light.

What a beautiful display!

Think of a time that you saw an incredible rainbow. Did you tell others to look?

Did you enjoy it yourself in your heart?

Day 7

I can't wait for ___________!

This may be something that you've been working toward or something that you're envisioning enjoying. Imagine that moment.

How will you feel when you ___________?

What will be happening?

Day 8

Remember a moment when you had little cares. Was it sunny or cloudy?

What did you hear?

What food did you eat?

Imagine that state of being. What one thing can you do today to be one step closer to that fabulous memory?

What one thing can you do to relieve one little piece of stress and be more care free?

Day 9

Imagine the most beautiful sunset you've seen. The sunset that made you stop what you were doing just to admire God's beautiful artwork for a moment.

Where did you experience this view?

What where you doing?

In your mind, describe and recreate the awe that you felt at that time in this moment.

Isn't it glorious?!

Day 10

What did you so look forward to as a child?

Was it a place?

Was it a person?

You couldn't wait to ___________!

What made you feel that way?

Imagine being a child again and reliving that very experience now. Is there a similar experience you could recreate and share with someone at this stage in life that may treasure it as much as you did?

Day 11

Remember an experience that was filled with such beauty that it brought tears to your eyes.

What was it?

What where your surroundings like?

How incredibly beautiful!

Day 12

What happened in the last month that was so funny that you belly-laughed?

Who was involved?

What was the context?

Are you laughing now?

If others were involved, take the opportunity to call them and let them know that you were just thinking of them and remembering the funny moment you shared together.

Day 13

Who said something positive about you that surprised you?

Might it have been something you doubted in yourself that someone admires?

Imagine how you felt when they made that comment.

Day 14

Imagine the pride of completing a task that you thought might never happen. As you step back (in your mind's eye of course), to admire your accomplishment, imagine the pride you have deep down in your heart. You did it!

What do you have on your plate now that will provide a similar, maybe even greater sense of pride and accomplishment when complete?

Get after it and make it happen!

You've already had incredible accomplishments in the past. You clearly have history of making things possible.

What a great feeling!

Day 15

I can't wait to __________!

Are you going somewhere or doing an activity?

Have you achieved something in your mind that you intend to achieve in real life in the future?

Imagine that excitement and pride!

Day 16

What non-human living thing did you last look at that made you smile?

Was it a plant?

Was it an animal?

What where the circumstances that brought a smile to your face?

Day 17

I magine the adorable thing that a child said about or to you.

Isn't it heartwarming how innocent and honest young children are?

Knowing it was exactly what they were thinking at the time does, the memory bring a smile to your face?

Day 18

You told someone something that turned their entire outlook around. The negative they were experiencing suddenly stopped. Your words or actions gave them purpose and a positive outlook in that moment.

What was it?

Day 19

Won't it be incredible when ___________!

What can I do today to be one step closer to making it reality?

Day 20

I magine your power look. You know, the outfit and hair/makeup that you feel like you can own a room. You look like you can conquer the world! Imagine the strength of your walk. Imagine how others perceive your confidence.

When was the last time you had your power look going on?

Is that how you look now? If not, when you wake up tomorrow put it on. Go all in because you own your look and feelings about yourself. Even if you don't leave the house, each time you pass a mirror, pause for a moment, smile at yourself and appreciate the powerful person you are and know that this is your day to shine!

Day 21

Imagine your favorite season. This season makes your heart sing.

What do the temperatures feel like?

What smells are in the air?

What makes you love it so?

Day 22

Have you seen a shooting star? It's so special because they exist for only an instant; a small moment in time and then they're gone.

If you were lucky enough to have witnessed one how excited were you?

If you haven't looked up for a while, go outside and do some stargazing. Can you find the Big Dipper?

Day 23

Describe a moment that was so incredible that it took your words away.

There was nothing to say. It was all about being in the moment and you didn't want to miss a thing.

Day 24

Remember the time when someone said you did something well that you weren't expecting.

How flattering!

Even those little things we discount in ourselves are huge in other's eyes.

Day 25

Imagine the cutest little animal. Isn't it so adorable?!

Does it walk?

Does it swim?

What makes it so sweet?

Day 26

Imagine a scent you so enjoy that isn't perfume. What is it?

Where or when can someone appreciate that aroma?

What makes it so meaningful to you?

Day 27

Sometimes words just come out perfectly. Remember the last time you made a witty comment.

Did you get a reaction from those around you or perhaps a little chuckle that you enjoyed yourself?

Isn't it great how these little memories can still make us smile today?

Day 28

Think of someone who admires you.

What quality do they see in you that they'd like to see in themselves?

Reach out to them today with a word of encouragement. It will make their day to hear from you!

Day 29

Imagine the warmth of ___________.

It's such a nice feeling.

When was the last time you felt and experienced it?

Day 30

Think of one moment today made you feel good.

What happened?

Where were you at the time?

Day 31

Have you been blessed with a complete stranger doing something for you that they didn't have to?

How great it is to be the one "paying it forward" and seeing the smile on the face of the unsuspecting recipient!

Smiles are contagious so be sure to make someone smile and in return you may just find yourself smiling too.

Did You Know

You are an example.

Someone is looking up to you.

Someone is watching you achieve your next goal. When you do, they'll see that it might just be possible for them to reach theirs too.

You're such an inspiration!

You've come so far.

People you would never expect are proud of your successes and the obstacles you've overcome.

You don't have to move fast. You just have to move.

You've got this!

Just keep going!

Affirmations

What is your daily mantra? Take a moment to affirm your life and "Speak your affirmations into existence." You may wish to print these, write your own, and place them in a prominent area that you can't help but see on a regular basis like a bathroom mirror perhaps. This is your positive daily practice.

I am happy.

I am blessed.

I am healthy.

I am strong.

I am confident.

I am joyful.

I am grateful.

I am admired.

People love me.

I have so much love in my heart.

I radiate happiness.

Opportunities seek me out.

Money comes to me.

I am making moves each day that put me one step closer to where I want to be.

I love my life!

Daily Smiles

I f you're ready to make a positive change in your heart, mind and spirit, utilize these exercises daily and you'll find that smiling will come naturally. Begin your day with your Affirmations then conclude the day with a Self-Reminder. Do this consistently. Yes, by consistently, I mean every day. Those days when you're just not "in the mood," are usually the days that you will benefit most. It may be a struggle at first and that's okay. Keep doing it! In time, it will become more natural and your confidence and happiness will grow in leaps and bounds.

Have faith and know that each day is getting better, brighter, more joyous and will continue so long as you continue to invite the positive you seek in your life.

When you return to begin your next practice of your 31 Self-Reminders tomorrow, next week, next month or even years to come you'll find that your answers may differ from the last time you went through each. That's great. You are ALWAYS growing as a person.

Know with absolute certainty that challenges have not only made you stronger, but they've given you talking points; stories that others can relate to and understand from. Challenges and obstacles make us the humans we are. Everyone experiences down days even if it's not visible on social media or television.

If not for those challenges, we'd seem too-good-to-be-true. Embrace each challenge, each obstacle, each stumbling block and know that you'll overcome it in time. Just keep pressing forward. Keep the faith. There will come a day when you look back with pride about how far you've come.

Remember others are looking on and inspired by each little win you have.

Closing

Isn't it nice to think about all the large and small joys in life? When we pause to reflect, we realize that each year, each month, each week, and even down to each day is filled with tiny, little, happy moments. Let's stop a moment and be thankful for each, and remember that we have so many more happy moments to look forward to in our future.

At the end of the day, happiness is a choice we make. Decide today to find the happy in each day and you'll find yourself smiling more and more ;)

Resources

Luke 12 (NIV). (n.d.). Bible Gateway. Retrieved 29 October 2022, from https://www.biblegateway.com/passage/?search=luke +12